THE **TESTING** SERIES

PL NNING EXERCISES
FOR THE ARMED FORCES

THE **TESTING** SERIES
expert advice on test preparation

how2become

Orders: Please contact How2become Ltd, Suite 2, 50 Churchill Square Business Centre, Kings Hill, Kent ME19 4YU.

Telephone: (44) 0845 643 1299 – Lines are open Monday to Friday 9am until 5pm. Fax: (44) 01732 525965. You can also order via the e-mail address info@ how2become.co.uk.

ISBN: 9781909229587

First published 2014

Typeset for How2become Ltd by Molly Hill, Canada.

Printed in Great Britain for How2become Ltd by CMP (uk) Limited, Poole, Dorset

INTRODUCTION

During the selection process for Army Officer, RAF Officer and Royal Navy Officer you will be required to undertake a Planning Exercise session. In order to prepare effectively we strongly advise that you take the time to gradually work through the following 8 exercises. At the end of the workbook there are sample solutions to each exercise. However please be advised that our sample solutions do not necessarily represent the most efficient and quickest solution, please use them as guidance only. Please note that the following exercises will not be the same as the one you will be required to sit at your actual assessment; however, they are a great way to prepare.

Allow yourself 1 hour per exercise.

Disclaimer: Any Names, characters, places and incidents are either the product of the author's imagination, or are used fictitiously. Any resemblance to actual persons, living or dead, business establishments, events, or places is entirely coincidental

For more titles that will help you prepare for the Armed Forces selection process please visit **www.how2become.com**

PLANNING EXERCISE 1
SEASIDE MISSION

You are the duty officer in charge at the Royal National Lifeboat Institution's (RNLI) rescue centre at FLITTERBY. The FLITTERBY lifeboat is currently involved in rescuing some sailors from a drifting yacht in the Irish Sea.

It is exactly 10:00 am and the coxswain of the lifeboat has just radioed the following message to you:

"One of the sailors we have taken off from the sinking yacht is desperately ill and must have a blood transfusion as soon as possible. I have just been talking, by radio, to the Accident & Emergency (A&E) staff at ASHBY hospital and they will be standing-by to receive him but have pointed out that every minute counts. Make sure the RNLI's ambulance (a specially adapted estate car) is ready to take him to the hospital as soon as we arrive at the jetty. I cannot give you an exact time of arrival, but it will not be before 10:20 hours, or later than 10:45 hours. Once we are tied up, it will take us 5 minutes to get him from the boat into the ambulance. It will be up to you to get him from the jetty to the A&E dept with the utmost urgency."

You study the map and recollect that there are 3 ways to get to hospital, each with advantages and disadvantages:

1. The route via the gate bridge is subject to delays as the crossings are controlled and the bridge is only open 3 times per hour for 12 minutes. The bridge is open at 10 minutes past, 30 minutes past and 10 minutes to the hour. The journey across the gate bridge will take you 10 minutes. The B120 is twisty and a maximum average speed could be no greater than 30 mph.

2. The route through the centre of ASHBY on the A424 is further but although it should be possible to average 40 mph out of town, once inside the central congestion zone, heavy traffic and narrow streets mean no more than 15 mph can be averaged for the 2 miles through the walled part of the town. The one limitation in using the A424 is that from 11:00 hrs onwards the central congestion zone is very dense and traffic is at a standstill.

3. The new A11 by-pass is dual carriage and passes the hospital but, although the longest route, will allow averages of 60 mph to be achieved. It is possible to reach the A11 from FLITTERBY in 10 mins.

4. You warn the duty driver to stand-by. Unfortunately, you cannot alert the local police on the telephone to make any special arrangements, so there is no way of interrupting the steady but reliable timetable of the gate bridge. The duty officer at nearby RAF Valley tells you the Search and Rescue helicopter is unavailable as it is on a mission rescuing someone from an oil rig miles out at sea.

After evaluating the information received, your task is to deliver the stricken sailor to the hospital in the quickest possible time?

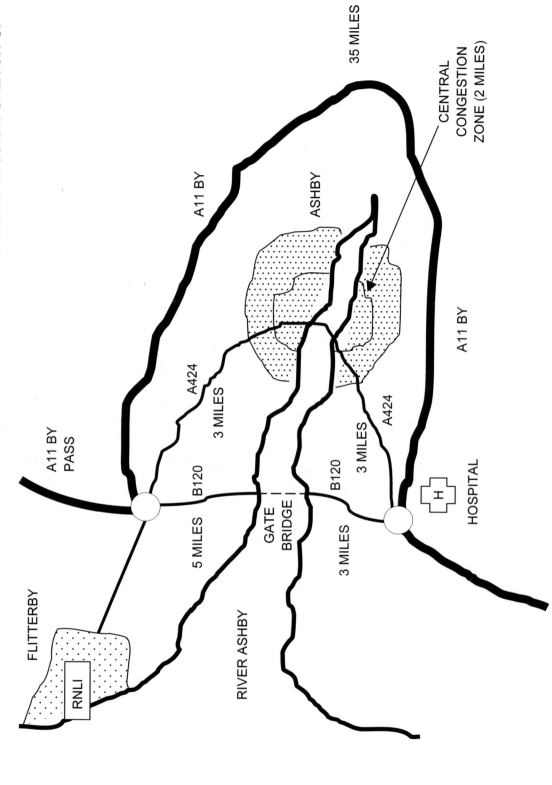

SEASIDE MISSION SKETCH UP

35 MILES

CENTRAL CONGESTION ZONE (2 MILES)

A11 BY

ASHBY

A11 BY

A424

3 MILES

A11 BY PASS

FLITTERBY

RNLI

A424

3 MILES

B120

3 MILES

B120

5 MILES

GATE BRIDGE

3 MILES

H

HOSPITAL

RIVER ASHBY

IRISH SEA

PLANNING EXERCISE 2
SPANISH SUSPENSE

You are on an outward bound expedition in Spain with four others, Harry, Kevin, Mark and Jeremy. Four of you are at your base camp (see map) relaxing and preparing a meal after a hard day's climbing at Fuentetoba Rocks which are four miles from the base camp over rough country. The fifth member of your party, Jeremy, is away on foot looking for a good climb for the following day.

Jeremy arrives back at camp, breathless and agitated. He explains that as he crossed the bridge over El Passo River, 2 miles to the East of the base camp, he noticed that a large tree is damaged, leaning at an angle and likely to fall on the bridge and demolish it. He could not do anything about it by himself, but reckons 3 men with ropes could pull the tree away from the bridge within 10 minutes. He points to the battered old Land Rover that you have hired for the trip and suggests that one man could pull the tree clear using the vehicle. You know that the bridge is the only means of access to the remote hamlet, Ardales, and therefore very important to the small community. Jeremy confesses that he is no expert on damaged trees, but he estimates that unless something is done about it, the tree will probably fall on the bridge in an hour's time.

All 5 of you gather up your climbing ropes and are about to head off to the bridge in the Land Rover when a girl staggers into the camp. You recognise her as Sarah, one of the climbers that you met at Fuentetoba rocks earlier that day, when you left they were about to tackle a particularly difficult climb. Sarah has injured her shoulder, she is bleeding from a bad cut on her head and she is in shock. She blurts out that her companion, Johnny, fell off the rock and is badly hurt; she has made him as comfortable as possible at the foot of the rock. Sarah is a medical student and she believes Johnny needs expert medical attention involving an operation within the next 4 hours. Having explained exactly where Johnny is, she passes out.

As you have attended a Pre RCB at Strensall and it is known that you did well, the others in the group look at you as their natural leader. They chorus "what are we to do?"

Your brain racing, you review the situation. You decide that Sarah should not be left alone, while unconscious. The nearest hospital is at Malaga, 20 miles from your base camp along a rough track. You know that there is Range Rover ambulance there which can do 40mph on the tracks and 6mph across country. Your hired Land Rover can manage 15 mph on tracks and 3mph across country. All your party are quite fit and can achieve 4 mph on the tracks and 3 mph across country. You work out that 4 men could carry an injured man at 2mph, but 2 men could only manage 1 mph.

What are you going to do?

SPANISH SUSPENSE SKETCH MAP

FUENTETOBA ROCKS

JOHNNY

4 MILES

BASE CAMP

2 MILES

THE BRIDGE

TO ARDALES

EL PASSO RIVER

TRACK

TO MALAGA

(20 MILES FROM BASE CAMP)

PLANNING EXERCISE 3
LOGISTIC MAJESTIC

You are the dispatcher and driver for an Army Military Transport Unit based at UPSHOT BARRACKS (see attached map). Your normal operating hours are from 07:30 hours to whenever the last job is completed. However, this evening your Commanding Officer wants all members of the unit, in uniform, for a photograph at 17:05 hrs. Nonetheless, the unit directive requires that all requests for same-day transport received before 15:00 hours be met; after that time, tasks will be held over for the following day.

With 2 tasks left to complete today and the 15:00 hours deadline approaching, the telephone rings. A Royal Engineer, not affiliated to your unit is needed urgently at Garrick Barracks outside the town and he needs to take a large, bulky tank part with him. A lack of fuel, due to a petrol tanker drivers' strike, means that he can only get as far as your office so he needs onward travel; he will be with you any moment now and he expects to stay at Garrick barracks for 45 minutes. You already have a 150kg package to collect from one of your regular customers, a supply depot in RIGBY, to be delivered to the barracks next door to your office, and the wife of the Commanding Officer needs to be collected from home in HAMPTON by 15:25 hours to attend a civic reception in the Town Hall opposite the office at 15:45 hours.

Due to other tasks, the only vehicles now available to you are an estate car similar to that used by the specialist engineer and with 30 litres of fuel in the tank, a small truck with 17 litres and a courier motorcycle complete with panniers with 9 litres. In addition to you there are 2 other drivers available. The previously mentioned petrol strike means no further fuel is available. The estate car can average 30 mph at 2½ miles/litre; the truck can average 40 mph at 5 miles/litre and the motorcycle averages 50mph at 10miles/litre. You also know that major road-works south of the town will add 20 minutes to the direct journey between UPSHOT and RIGBY.

By the time you complete your plan and brief the other drivers it will be 15:00 hours. Find a solution that allows all tasks to be completed in the allotted time.

LOGISTIC MAJESTIC SKETCH MAP

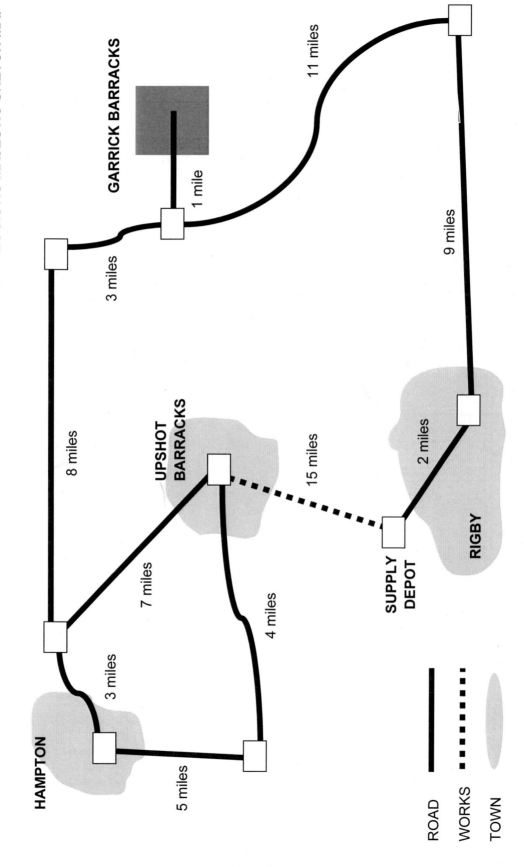

PLANNING EXERCISE 4
LOCKED UP

SITUATION

1. The 2 countries, TENYA and SENYA (see attached sketch map), have been at war for 2 years. TENYA received reliable reports of a considerable build up of stores and equipment in Mumba Town, SENYA, in preparation for an invasion of TENYA. The invasion is planned for 26th June.

2. The bulk of these stores are being moved by means of extensive canal networks from the neighbouring neutral country of RENYA. Apart from the canal system there is no other means of bulk transportation in SENYA.

3. You are a specialist demolition expert serving with TENYIAN Rifles based in the Capital city of Tenya, Lock Town. On 23 June you are briefed as follows:

"The SENYIANS are expected to mount an invasion of TENYA on the 26 June. It is imperative that we delay this invasion for at least 48 hours from 23:59 hours June 25. Intelligence reports indicate that this can be achieved if the supply of stores from RENYA is stopped by putting the canal system out of action for this period. It is your task to achieve this."

PERSONNEL & STORES

4. To assist you in your task you are given a group consisting of 1 sergeant, who is the demolition expert, and 6 men.

5. The following equipment is at your disposal:

   A. Explosive – 100 lbs

   B. Detonators – Sufficient for 4 demolitions.

   C. Rations – Sufficient for 7 days

   D. Radios – 2 small, portable short range radios

LOCKS

6. The following amounts of explosive are required to demolish the locks:

Lock A	90 lbs	**Lock B**	100 lbs
Lock C	40 lbs	**Lock D**	80 lbs
Lock E	90 lbs	**Lock F**	50 lbs
Lock G	50 lbs		

7. It will take at least 4 hours to prepare each lock for demolition. Locks A, B and E require 6 men to prepare the demolition, the remainder require only 3 men.

8. Lock A, on the frontier with RENYA is the only one guarded, probably by an infantry platoon. Once demolished it would be a matter of months before it would be repaired.

9. Some of the Platoon from Lock A, patrol Lock B every 2 hours, from 0600hrs till 0000hrs, they stay for 20 minutes, then return to Lock A. If destroyed the Lock would take at least 48 hours to repair after demolition.

10. The remaining locks are not guarded. Each would take a minimum of 48 hours to repair after demolition. In the event of the alarm being raised enemy patrols could be on the lock in a few minutes.

11. Demolitions must be prepared after dark. It is essential to reconnoitre the locks during daylight. There is plenty of cover surrounding each lock to avoid detection during daylight hours

GENERAL

12. Your party will be taken by motor launch to any point on the SENYIAN coast you wish, where you will rendezvous (RV) with friendly guides. These guides will also assist your escape and will leave a contact at the RV until 06:00 hours on the June 29.

13. It is essential to travel only at night, on foot and to avoid any contact with the local population, other than your guides. On no account should any attempts be made to steal bicycles, cars etc as would only raise the alarm.

14. Although RENYA is neutral, the armed forces of both TENYA and SENYA are unwelcome and treated as hostile.

15. Your party are all fit and can maintain a speed of 2 miles in every hour, at night, for long distances over SENYA terrain.

16. First light is 06:00 hours. Last light is 18:00 hours. There is no moon.

17. Based on available information, you decide to demolish the lock at E and set off for an RV with the guides at point X on the SENYIAN coast. Your estimated time of arrival (ETA) is 05:00 hours 24th June.

SITUATION UPDATE

18. Unfortunately, the compass of the motor launch was faulty and you are dropped in the wrong place.

19. It is now 09:00 hours 24th June, you and your party are lying up under cover at point Y. You have all your stores with the exception of the radios which were left behind on the launch.

20. You have no means of direct contact with the guides at point X and so cannot inform them of the situation.

21. You study your map and estimate the following distances:

From Y to:		To x from:	
Lock A	22 miles	**Lock A**	68 miles
Lock B	20 miles	**Lock B**	59 miles
Lock C	22 miles	**Lock C**	57 miles
Lock D	23 miles	**Lock D**	50 miles
Lock E	37 miles	**Lock E**	14 miles
Lock F	14 miles	**Lock F**	47 miles
Lock G	22 miles	**Lock G**	48 miles
		Point Y	33 miles

REQUIREMENTS

22. Write down your thought process in arriving at a plan in such a form that anyone reading it would be able to understand how you had arrived at your plan and exactly what your plan would be.

LOCKED UP SKETCH MAP

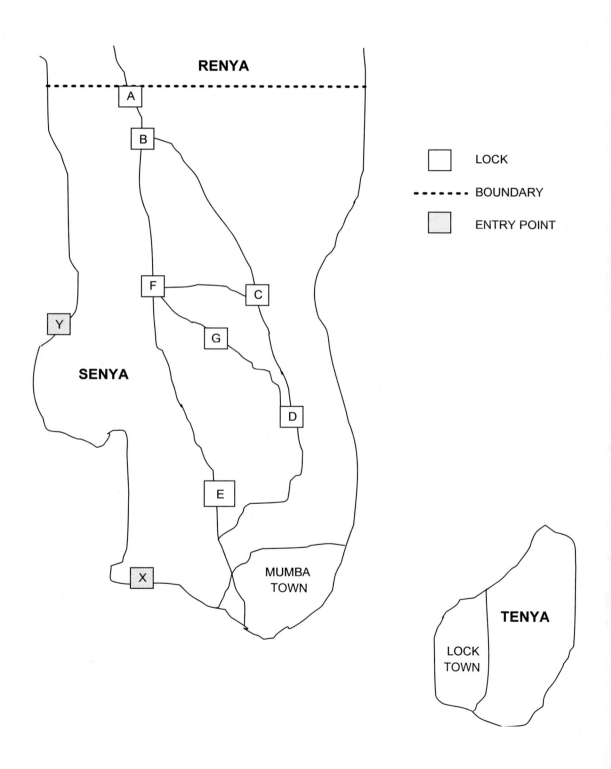

RENYA

A

B

F   C

Y   G

SENYA   D

E

X   MUMBA
TOWN

LOCK

BOUNDARY

ENTRY POINT

TENYA

LOCK
TOWN

PLANNING EXERCISE 5
EARTHQUAKE RESCUE

1. You are a member of the local mountain rescue team and are visiting your parents at their home in WODSWORTH (see sketch map). In the early hours of the morning you receive a telephone call on your mobile phone from the mountain rescue teams leader, who informs you that a huge earthquake has caused devastation on the welsh border and all mountain rescue teams are going to help in casualty evacuation and searching for survivors. You are the only qualified team medic available and the team leader needs you to report to the local bus station where rescue teams from around the region are being collected by coach and transported to the earthquake site. To make sure that you catch the coach, you would have to meet the team at MELTON local bus station. The coach departs at 10:18 hours today and it is imperative you are there. He also tells you that lives are at risk if you are not there in time.

2. You immediately realise that some of your equipment including your rucksack is at your parent's home. Your rucksack is in the cupboard but you have lent your climbing ropes and clothing to your cousin who lives in KINTON; you know that he has no equipment of his

own and would need a rucksack to carry your ropes and equipment over any distance. You last spoke to him on your phone yesterday and he told you he would be at home today. Your climbing boots are awaiting your collection from the repair shop at FENBY and a new medic pack is awaiting your collection from the local hospital in GRANGETHORPE. You want to collect the boots yourself because you need to make sure that they have fitted your boots correctly. It is also important that you collect the medical supplies yourself as they will not give it out to anyone other than you. You know from experience that you cannot expect to be served in any of the shops or the hospital in less than 10 minutes.

3.   You realise that, by the time you have made your plan, it will be 08:30 hours. Your Father, the only other member of your family with you in the house, has just left on his motorbike to complete a local errand and will not be back until 08:35 hours. He will be leaving the house again on his motorbike at 08:50 hours and will pass your cousin's house on his way to work in BIDDLESTOCK. He collects a work colleague en route and so he cannot be diverted from his schedule. His motor bike can average 40 mph over the local roads. You consult the bus time table and find that there is only one bus that could be of any use. It stops at WODSWORTH at 09:18 hours, the Queen Victoria public house (PH on map) at 09:35 hours and GRANGETHORPE at 09:40 hours. You have a bicycle on which you know you can average 12 mph, regardless of what you are carrying, but you would never consider leaving it for an extended period, other than safely locked up at home or in the custody of a friend. A person could expect to average no more than 4 mph when walking on local roads.

4.   You know it will take 10 minutes to collect your personal belongings from your parents and pack them into your rucksack, another of those important tasks you always do yourself.

5.   Write down your thought process in arriving at a plan in such a form that anyone reading it would be able to understand how you had arrived at your plan and exactly how long your plan will take.

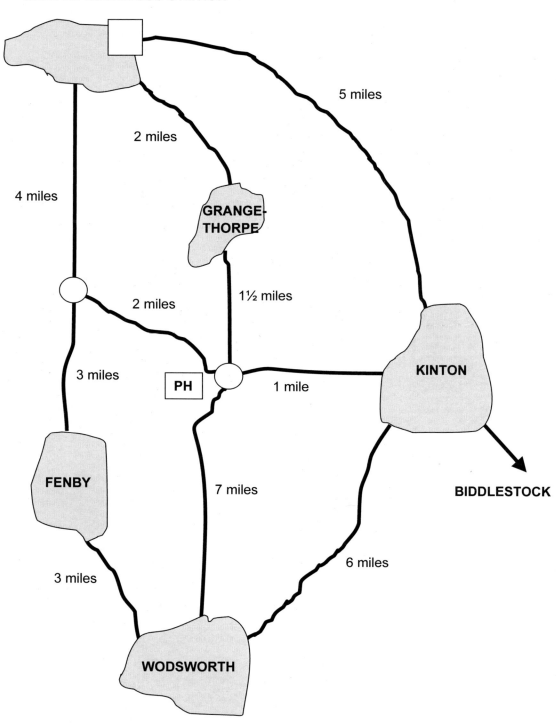

EARTHQUAKE MISSION
SKETCH MAP

MELTON LOCAL BUS STATION

5 miles

2 miles

4 miles

GRANGE-THORPE

1½ miles

2 miles

3 miles

PH

1 mile

KINTON

BIDDLESTOCK

FENBY

7 miles

3 miles

6 miles

WODSWORTH

PLANNING EXERCISE 6
TURKIC DELIGHT

You are a member of a student expedition which plans to make an overland journey across the Kara-Kum desert in Turkmenistan carrying out archaeological and geographical studies on the way. You are particularly glad to be taking part in the expedition as it is vital that you obtain first-hand knowledge of the Kara-Kum which will form an important part of the thesis you are preparing for your final examinations.

The party assembles at YERBENT, a developed town in Kara-Kum region bordered by the Aral Sea to the North West. It is decided that the pack will split into two independent groups for the first part of the expedition, proceeding by different routes to the oasis of HAJI QUSHAN which is about 200 miles south of YERBENT. From HAJI QUSHAN the remainder of the expedition will be carried out as a joint enterprise; because of the ever-present threat of bandits it is considered too dangerous for one group acting alone to make the hazardous journey across the LEBAP (southern) region. It is agreed that the two groups will meet at HAJI QUSHAN by July 15; if one group fails to arrive by that date the remainder of the expedition will be cancelled and the group at HAJI QUSHAN will move off at 08:00 hours on the July 16 to return to YERBENT by the same route it used to arrive there.

As you have played an important part in planning the expedition, you are put in charge of one group which consists of yourself, and six others. Your transport is a minibus and you are supplied with food, oil and petrol as well as lightweight camping equipment and geographical apparatus. One of the men in your group is an enthusiastic amateur car mechanic and will be responsible for keeping the minibus in good order during the expedition. None of the group can speak Arabic but one of the students is a linguist and speaks fluent French and Italian.

Before leaving YERBENT you call at the local government offices for advice about your journey. You are informed that the main roads of the country are well surfaced and that it is possible to average 30 mph on them during the day; care must be taken at night but the road is still usable. The tracks off the main roads are not really designed for wheeled traffic as the surface is very uneven and loose sand makes progress difficult. Land Rovers are the most suitable vehicles for use on tracks but even these find it difficult to average more than 5 mph. You point out that your party will be using a minibus and are told that it will still be possible to use tracks but that extreme caution will be necessary.

The local official advises you that there are police posts in the interior and that the police are always ready to help foreign travellers if they require assistance. You are warned, however, that few native policemen speak English although most of them understand Italian. The final advice which is offered to you is to take plentiful supplies of fresh water as, at this time of the year, some of the drinking wells have dried up.

The minibus is equipped with a large fresh water tank which you consider will be more than adequate for the journey to HAJI QUSHAN where, you are assured, there is a constant supply of fresh water.

You leave YERBENT on schedule and plan to arrive at HAJI QUSHAN on the 14th of July. The first part of the journey goes smoothly except that your friend, Kelly Smith, contracts dysentery. By the time you arrive in BUKHARA, on the morning of the 14th, she is clearly in need of rest and since you are now less than 50 miles from HAJI QUSHAN you decide to camp at ZIMDA and to make an early start for HAJI QUSHAN the next morning.

Some British Army troops, equipped with light trucks and Land Rovers, are exercising in the area and have set up their base one mile north of BUKHARA. You camp in the same area. Later that day you meet a group of officers who have been taking part in an exercise. You learn that the exercise will end at 07:00 hours on the morning of July 16, when the troops will strike camp and move back North.

The officers you talk to are very interested in your expedition and make an offer of any assistance should you require it. They warn you that the local people of BUKHARA are unfriendly; normally they will not molest you but in view of their attitude and the danger of bandits it is essential to move in pairs at least, particularly at night on the tracks. The officer also warns you that the DAMLA-CHINABED-HAJI QUSHAN area contains unexploded minefields laid by the Germans and Italians during the last war. It is very dangerous to wander from the roads and tracks as a mine can be detonated by treading on it. Mines have been triggered off by unwary travellers less than two feet from the edge of the tracks. The tracks are not well defined and impossible to follow at night so you are strongly advised to stay put in camp during the hours of darkness, once you leave the main road at DAMLA. It is reasonably safe to travel on the main road at night.

Next morning you are relieved to find Kelly is recovering and is fit to travel. However, when your driver comes to start the minibus he discovers that the engine is dead. Your mechanic is unable to trace the fault and finally you call on the Army for assistance. They are sympathetic and promise to send over a mechanic as soon as one reports in from this morning's exercise. It is not until midday, and by now very hot, that a mechanic becomes available. He quickly diagnoses the fault as a defective petrol pump. He is able to repair the pump and assures you that it should give you no further problems.

You finally leave BUKHARA at 13:30 hours with the intention of proceeding non-stop to HAJI QUSHAN. The road from BUKHARA to DAMLA is a good one and you get to DAMLA by 14:30 hours noting, as you pass, that the wells are still usable although the oasis appears deserted. Once you take the track south of DAMLA the going becomes extremely rough. The track is deeply rutted and the driver has to keep a sharp eye open for rocks in his path. Deep sand fills the hollows and, on numerous occasions, the party has to dismount to push the vehicle out of the sand. By 16:00 hours you are only five miles south of DAMLA and; with some distance to go before you arrive at the main road leading to HAJI QUSHAN, you begin to get anxious as you have only three hours of daylight left.

Suddenly, as this goes through your mind, the minibus hits a deep crevasse and Keels over alarmingly. Everyone gets out to manhandle the vehicle on to level ground but the weight of it is too much and it crashes over on its side, trapping one of the party, Parry underneath. Quickly, you organise the unloading of the equipment until it is possible to position the minibus upright and on level ground again, freeing Parry in the process.

One of your party is a medical student and examines Parry, the injured man. He informs you that Parry appears to have crushed his ankle and is probably suffering from concussion. He can be given temporary first aid but should receive expert medical attention as soon as possible. There is no possibility of Parry being able to continue with the expedition.

While Parry is being examined you find that the water tank in the minibus fractured in the accident and that all the fresh water has been lost except for a half gallon container which is half full. At this stage the medical student points that water will be required for both Parry and Kelly by 10:00 hours or dehydration will take place in the heat.

Your mechanic inspects the damage to the vehicle and states that the suspension is broken. It is not possible to move the vehicle any further. He will try and mend the damage but it will take a long time and it will not be possible to work on it in the dark. A rough estimate is that it is unlikely to be ready before 08:00-09:00 hours in the morning and then it will need particularly careful driving.

You look at the map. There are still eight miles of track ahead before you reach the junction with the main road, three miles north of HAJI QUSHAN. There is a police post at CHINABAD which is 12 miles by track from DAMLA; CHINABAD is 25 miles (by road) north of HAJI QUSHAN. BUKHARA is 26 miles north of DAMLA but the road carries very little traffic. You estimate that, on foot, it will be possible to average 2 mph on track and 3 mph on the roads. First light is at 05:00 hours.

REQUIREMENT

Write down your thought process in arriving at a plan which will provide assistance to the injured and other members of your group, and how you will inform the second party.

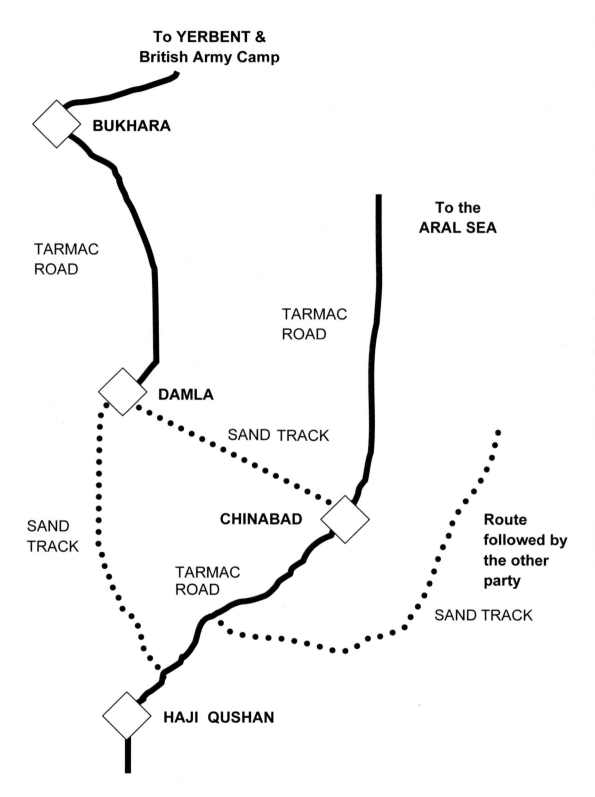

PLANNING EXERCISE 7
COLUMBUS COUNTDOWN

You are a passenger on a chartered airline flying home to visit family in South America. There are 19 passengers onboard in total: 16 men (including you), 2 women and 1 child (MEREDITH). You departed from Heathrow at 06:00 GMT.

Five hours into the flight you see fire coming from the starboard engine. Looking at an atlas (which you always have when flying) you ascertain that you're over Columbus Island and it seems the pilot is descending. The engines go dead and the pilot tells the crew and passengers to brace for a forced landing. You scramble out of the wreckage of the aircraft and you can see that all the passengers are fine besides being in shock. However, when you look in the cockpit you discover that the captain is dead and the co-pilot has a concussion.

You grab all the supplies of food and water you can before the aircraft bursts into flames. You also managed to find a flare gun and rounds. You calculate that the supplies will last the group approximately 24 hours. You look around and notice that you are in an isolated, uninhabited mountainous area. Using the crew members' radio you manage to contact the American Coastguard operating in the area. They inform you that they will only be able to take 3 passengers and will not be at your location for another 3 ¼ hours. After the transmission the batteries go dead and you can't get the radio working again.

In the distance you see a local farmer and he informs you that the area is very dangerous because a local bandit named MANUEL is operating in the vicinity with his gang of 8 men. The farmer tells you that Manuel's gang is ruthless and will rob and kill any travellers they come across. He informs you that they are armed with pistols but will not attack a group twice their size when over 2 miles away from their hideout. However, they will attack any group that is static of any size. You ask where Manuel is now and the farmer tells you that he is currently in the Village of VICTORIA and is not due back at the hideout until 13:30 hours local time. A friend of Manuel has seen the crash and is on his way to inform him and they are likely to take advantage of the crash straight away. Just before the farmer disappears he draws you a sketch map of the area, explaining that a dirt road linking VICTORIA and GARCIA has been absolutely destroyed by an earthquake but a subsequent path has been trodden where it used to be by local shepherds.

With information from the farmer and observations you can ascertain that:

A. GMT is 1 hour behind local time

B. The country is vast and the only way to travel to the villages would be on the paths, tracks and roads.

C. Speeds:

Manuel's Gang		Our Group	
Track	2 mph	Track	1 mph
Paths	1 mph	Paths	½ mph
Dirt Roads	4 mph	Dirt Roads	2 mph

D.   Distances:

Point X (Crash Site) to	Point Y	1/2 mile
Point Y to	Victoria	5 miles
Point Y to	Columbo	7 miles
Point Y to	Garcia	7 miles
Point Y to	Point B	1 mile
Point Y to	Point C	2 miles
Point Y to	Point E	1 mile
Point Y to	Point Z (Manuel's hideout)	2 mile
Point Z to	Point A	1 mile
Point Z to	Point B	2 miles
Point Z to	Point D	2 ½ miles
Point B to	Point D	1 ½ miles
Point E to	Point A	1 mile

E.   There are doctors at Victoria, Columbo and Garcia

UPDATE: As you're looking at the sketch map, Meredith's mother runs over to you in distress. She tells you that Meredith is a diabetic and needs to see a doctor to get some insulin as soon as possible.

With the captain dead and the co-pilot concussed the group start to discuss who will lead them to safety. The group decided that you would be the best leader as you have remained calm, gained as much information as possible and appear to be the natural leader of the group.

With this in mind, plan a solution so that anyone reading your plan would be able to follow it to the end.

COLUMBUS COUNTDOWN
SKETCH MAP

DIRT ROAD

TRACK

PATH

Victoria

Manuel's Hideout

Mountainous Area

Columbo

Crash site

A

E

Y

B

D

C

Victoria Forest

Garcia

PLANNING EXERCISE 8
BAY BLAZE

You live at Thumb Farm, a small farm 21 miles from Bay Bridge in the Yellowstone National Park (see map). It has been a long, hot summer and you have had an excellent wheat crop and your wheat is safely gathered in. The water level in the Lake has fallen and the forests are dangerously dry. There is considerable concern in this heavily forested area and there is a forest fire alert in force.

This morning your wife took your youngest son and nephew to the Bus station at Pebble Creek; a small town 40 miles by road from Bay Bridge. The Boys are due to catch the 9:45 am train to Madison to visit your parents. Your wife also plans to do some shopping for herself and a neighbour, Mrs Johnson, while she is at Pebble Creek. Mr Johnson is in Madison hospital as a result of a car accident. Mrs Johnson, whose ankle was broken in the accident, is in plaster and is back at Fox Cottage with her six year old daughter and her aged mother who is helping out. Understandably she is presently without a car. The cottage is 12 miles from Bay Bridge and is at the end of the 3 mile track off the Whick road. Although it is only 3½ miles from the cottage to the Alum Creek track to the east, the ground down to the lake side is rocky and almost impassable.

After shopping your wife aims to arrive at the Johnsons cottage by lunch-time. You do not expect her home before 5pm.

Your eldest son and a friend from College have gone in your 4 × 4 to fish at the Sister Lakes. To get there they have driven 2 miles up the Pelican Creek track and then walked for 10 minutes up the footpath to the lakes. They have taken a picnic lunch with them.

You and your sheepdog are just about to leave your farm on your tractor (the only vehicle left at the farm) to visit your 500 sheep. This entails travelling down the road for 2 miles on the road and a further mile on the hill track. Suddenly you are aware of the smell of wood smoke on the freshening north easterly wind. At the same time you see a National Park Wardens vehicle approaching from Alum Creek. The vehicle stops in a cloud of dust. The driver, whom you know, calls out that there is a forest fire raging to the North East at the head of Alum Creek some 9 miles away. He and two others working nearby were too late to contain the fire and two of them are now suffering from burns and smoke inhalation. He, the driver, has decided to take them via a short-cut hill track to the cottage hospital in Pebble Creek. Just as he drives off he asks you to inform the Park Fire Warden in Hayden that the fire is spreading fast and advancing, by his reckoning, at about 3mph. He adds that by now it will be 1 mile from Fishing Bridge, and a further 2 miles from Sister lakes. He stresses that the fire must be checked and must not be allowed to spread to the main forest areas. He tells you to get cracking and get the vital warning to the authorities, but he departs before you think of telling him you have no telephone.

Some of your immediate thoughts are:

- It is now 9:30 am
- Your eldest son and friends are fishing at the Sister Lakes
- Mrs Johnson, her children and Mother will be in danger
- Your wife has the Family Ford Estate which averages 25 mph on roads and 15 mph on tracks. She is likely to drive past Thumb Bridge between noon and 12:30pm

Your son has a 4 × 4 which averages 20 mph on roads, 10 mph on tracks. The only way out of Pelican Creek by vehicle is by the road past your house. Your son can be relied upon to act sensibly in an emergency.

You have the tractor which normally has an average road and track speed of 10 mph, but at present, with the ancillary equipment attached, this speed must be halved, it will take 30 minutes to detach the equipment.

There is a farm track which leads from the farm for 3 miles down to the Thumb Lake where there is a boat in a boatshed. It would take you 15 minutes to row across the lake at this point. It would then take you 10 minutes to climb up the footpath to the cottage. The Johnsons have a telephone and there is a public call-box by the roadside at Thumb Bridge 16 miles away.

The low ground around your house is open fields, beyond the forest area there is mainly open grass field. If you could get your sheep down to the grassland near the farm they would be saved. You and your son can cover the ground at 3 mph if on a track. At this moment your random thoughts are disrupted by the arrival of a man and women carrying rucksacks, who approach and ask for directions to the Tower Springs which are 4 miles up Pelican Creek. You tell them of the forest fires. They become agitated and tell you that they were due to meet two friends at the springs on the previous day but they had been delayed. Their friends had said that they would probably stay there for a couple of days. The man and woman were worried that their friends would be at the falls and be in danger from the fire. You are surprised to hear about their friends as you have not seen them. Most campers in the area stop at your farm buy supplies for their journey. Knowing this, you consider that it is very possible they are at the springs.

REQUIREMENTS

Write down your thought process in arriving at a plan in such a format that anyone reading it would be able to understand how and why you had arrived at your plan and exactly what your plan was and how long it would take to carry out.

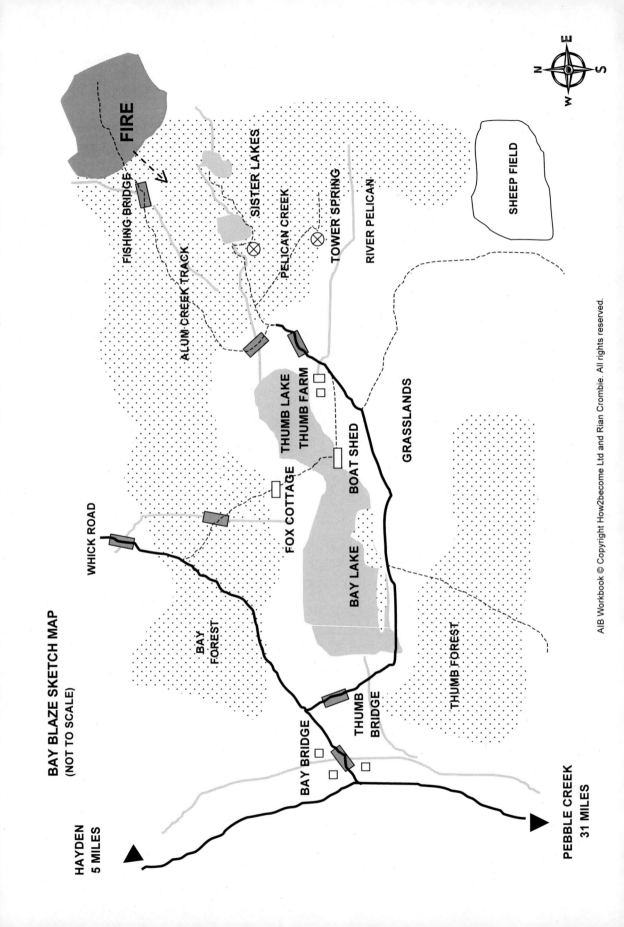

BAY BLAZE SKETCH MAP
(NOT TO SCALE)

HAYDEN
5 MILES

PEBBLE CREEK
31 MILES

FIRE

FISHING BRIDGE

SISTER LAKES

ALUM CREEK TRACK

PELICAN CREEK

TOWER SPRING

RIVER PELICAN

SHEEP FIELD

WHICK ROAD

BAY FOREST

FOX COTTAGE

THUMB LAKE

THUMB FARM

BOAT SHED

BAY LAKE

GRASSLANDS

THUMB FOREST

BAY BRIDGE

THUMB BRIDGE

POSSIBLE SOLUTIONS

PLANNING EXERCISE 1: SEASIDE MISSION SOLUTION

IMPORTANT! The following solutions are just examples of a possible way to complete the tasks in hand. They do not represent the most efficient or quickest way to complete the exercise, and should be used for guidance only.

AIMS

Transport the sailor to hospital as soon as possible for a blood transfusion.

OPTIONS

Option 1: Gate Bridge

Sailor arrives at 10:20 (earliest possibility)

Stage 1:

   a)   Loading sailor into ambulance = 5 minutes

   b)   Flitterby to A11 junction = 10 minutes

   c)   B120- 5 miles at 30 mph = 10 minutes

   d)   10:20 hrs plus 25 minutes = 10:45 hrs

   e)   Gate bridge opens 10:50 hrs (5 minute wait)   **Total = 30 minutes**

Stage 2:

   a)   10 minutes to cross gate bridge

   b)   B120 – 3 miles @ 30 mph = 6 minutes   **Total = 16 minutes**

Time at hospital = 11:06

Sailor arrives at 10:45 (latest possibility)

Stage 1:

f) Loading sailor into ambulance = 5 minutes

g) Flitterby to A11 junction = 10 minutes

h) B120 – 5 miles at 30 mph = 10 minutes

i) 10:45 hrs plus 25 minutes = 11:10 hrs

j) Gate bridge opens 11:10 hrs (0 minute wait)   **Total = 25 minutes**

Stage 2:

c) 10 minutes to cross gate bridge

d) B120 – 3 miles @ 30 mph = 6 minutes   **Total = 16 minutes**

Time at hospital = 11:26

Option 2: A424

Sailor arrives at 10:20 (earliest possibility)

a)   Loading sailor into ambulance = 5 minutes

b)   Flitterby to A11 junction = 10 minutes

c)   2 miles at 15 mph (through central congestion zone) = 8 minutes

d)   6 miles at 40 mph = 9 minutes   **Total = 32 minutes**

Time at hospital = 10:52 hrs

Sailor arrives at 10:45 (latest possibility)

a)   10:45 hrs plus 32 minutes

Time at hospital = 11:17 hrs (only if traffic is not at a standstill)

Option 3: A11 bypass

Sailor arrives at 10:20 (earliest possibility)

e)   Loading sailor into ambulance = 5 minutes

f)   Flitterby to A11 junction = 10 minutes

g) 35 miles at 60 mph = 35 minutes   **Total = 50 minutes**

Time at hospital = 11:10 hrs

Sailor arrives at 10:45 (latest possibility)

b) 10:45 hrs plus 50 minutes

Time at hospital = 11:35 hrs

The plan is:

Plan A: Sailor arrives between 10:20 and 10:32½ – option 2 A424 chosen

Plan B: Sailor arrives between 10:33 and 10:45- option 1 gate bridge chosen

Using the A424 is by far the fastest way to get the sailor to the hospital. However, the variability of the traffic conditions makes the option very risky post 10:32½ (27½ minutes to get from RNLI centre to outside congestion zone for a free run to the hospital) as you would be caught in traffic. Hence option 1 is chosen post 10:32½. Option 3 is ruled out as it is longer than both options considering all factors.

PLANNING EXERCISE 2: SPANISH SUSPENSE SOLUTION

IMPORTANT! The following solutions are just examples of a possible way to complete the tasks in hand. They do not represent the most efficient or quickest way to complete the exercise, and should be used for guidance only.

AIMS

The aims, in order of priority, are:

a) To get Johnny to hospital as soon as possible

b) To get medical attention for Sarah as soon as possible

c) To save the bridge over El Passo River

FACTORS

Time & Space

1. Land Rover

a) To get Johnny – 4 miles at 3mph = 1 hour 20 mins

b) To get Johnny to Base Camp from rocks = 1 hour 20 mins

c) Total time to get Johnny to Base Camp = 2 hours 40 mins

d) To get to bridge – 2 miles at 15mph = 8 mins

2. Range Rover

a) From Malaga to Base Camp – 20 miles at 40mph = 30 mins

b) Base Camp to Johnny – 4 miles at 6mph = 40 mins

3. Get Johnny to Base Camp without vehicle

  a) Walking to rocks – 4 miles at 3mph = 1 hour 20 mins

  b) Carrying Johnny

   1. 4 men – 4 miles at 2 mph = 2 hours

   2. 2 men – 4 miles at 1mph = 4 hours

4. Deductions from Time and Space

  a) For the Land Rover to pick up Johnny and take him to Malaga takes 4 hours

  b) Using the Land Rover to go direct to Malaga to alert the Range Rover to collect Johnny

   I. Land Rover to Malaga = 1 hour 20 mins

   II. Range Rover to Johnny = 1 hour 10 mins

   III. Johnny to hospital using Range Rover = 1 hour 10 mins

  c) If we try and carry Johnny to Base camp without a vehicle, the quickest we could get him there would be 3 hours 20 mins, longer than either (a) or (b) above. Not worth considering further.

  d) Using the Land Rover to go to the bridge first before going to Malaga adds 16mins travel time to say nothing of time spent sorting out the tree. Unacceptable.

Manpower Available

  1. If I am not to use the Land Rover to save the bridge, I need 3 men on foot, leaving me with 2 others.

  2. I need 1 man to drive the Land Rover whichever option I choose, leaving me with 1 man spare

Options Open

Option 1: Use only Land Rover, collecting Johnny and taking him to hospital. 3 men walk to bridge

Option 2: Land Rover direct to Malaga, with Range Rover collecting Johnny and taking him to hospital. 3 men walk to the bridge.

Choice of Options – Option 2 because:

a) It is 20 minutes quicker than Option 1

b) Sarah is not left alone and gets treatment quicker as she can go to the hospital in the Land Rover which arrives in 1 hour 20 mins rather than 4 hours in option 1

Plan

The plan is:

a) One man takes Land Rover direct to Malaga, taking Sarah with him.

b) 3 men walk to bridge and get there in 30 mins, leaving 30 mins for them to sort the tree out before it falls

c) The 5th member of my party walks to Johnny to give him whatever help and comfort that he can. He will be with Johnny in 1 hour 20 mins, 1 hour 10 mins before the Range Rover arrives and I consider that worthwhile.

PLANNING EXERCISE 3: LOGISTIC MAJESTIC SOLUTIONS

IMPORTANT! The following solutions are just examples of a possible way to complete the tasks in hand. They do not represent the most efficient or quickest way to complete the exercise, and should be used for guidance only.

AIM

All tasks need to be completed and all personnel present for the unit photo at 1705 hours.

FACTORS & PLAN

Estate cars movements

Estate car to Commanding Officer's house ETD 15:00 (10 miles at 30 mph = 20 mins).

- ETA 15:20 and departs at same time for Town Hall (another 10 miles at 30mph = 20 mins).
- ETA 15:40 (5 mins to spare unless departure was delayed to 15:05).

Estate car now departs to Garrick Barracks ETD 15:40 (19 miles at 30 mph = 38 mins)

- ETA 16:18, collects Royal engineer

Estate car returns to unit (19 miles at 30 mph = 38 mins)

- ETA 16:56

Trucks movements

Truck to Garrick Barracks with Royal Engineer ETD 15:00 (19 miles at 40 mph = 28 mins)

- ETA 15:28 – Royal Engineer will be ready to depart at 16:13

Truck to supply depot (via South East route) (23 miles at 40 mph = 34 mins)

- ETD 15:28 for supply depot
- ETA and ETD supply depot 16:03

Truck return to barracks via road works (15 miles at 40 mph – 22 mins)

- Add 20 mins for road works
- ETA 16:45

Motor cycle

If the Royal Engineer has fitted bulky tank part and has no part to return, he could be collected by the motor cycle and would not, therefore have the 4 min wait at Garrick Barracks. However, even his tools might not fit in the panniers.

Motor cycle to Garrick Barracks (ETD as required) (but at 15:50 if there was no wait by either party) (19 miles at 50 mph = 23 mins)

- ETA 16:13

Motor cycle back to Upshot Barracks (19 miles at 50 mph = 23 mins)

- ETA 16:36

OTHER SOLUTIONS

One option would be to send the motor cycle to the Station Commander's house, the Estate car to the depot and the truck to Garrick Barracks, where it waits for the engineer. The Station Commander would not be very happy with his wife being on a motor cycle, though! All 3 drivers are also used, so there is no one to take the orders for tomorrow's tasks.

A second option would be to take the engineer to Garrick Barracks by truck, which then drives on to the supply depot, returning to Garrick to pick up the engineer up by reverse route. The estate car could then be used for the Commanding Officer's wife. However, the truck would be late arriving back (ETA 17:06) and you are under orders to be ready for the photograph by 17:05.

PLANNING EXERCISE 4: LOCKED UP SOLUTION

IMPORTANT! The following solutions are just examples of a possible way to complete the tasks in hand. They do not represent the most efficient or quickest way to complete the exercise, and should be used for guidance only.

AIM

1. The aim is to delay the invasion of TENYA for 48 hours from 23:59 hours on the 25th of June. A secondary aim may be to reach point X and RV with guides by 06:00 hours on the 29th of June

FACTORS

2. Explosives

a) 100 lbs of explosive available and 4 detonators are available.

- Other resources permitting 4 locks may be destroyed

b)

Lock	Explosives Required	Remarks
A	90	
B	100	
F/C	90	
F/D	130	Only 100 lbs available
F/G/D	180	Only 100 lbs available
E	90	

- The demolition of locks F, G and D will not be considered any further
- The demolition of locks F and D will not be considered any further

3. Personnel

- A total of 8 men including 2 demolition experts are available
- There are sufficient personnel to blow up 2 locks at any one time

4. Targets – in order to achieve the aim SENYA must be denied the use of the canal system for 48 hours. The aim can be achieved by destroying locks either individually or as a combination:

a) Lock A

b) Lock B

c) Lock E or D

d) Locks F & G

e) Locks C & F

It can be seen that Lock G must be destroyed in combination with at least 2 other locks. However, there is insufficient explosive for this. Therefore, Lock G will not be considered any further as a potential target.

5. Timings

a) Time now is 09:00 hours on the 24th of June. The locks must be blown by 23:59 hours on the 25th of June

- There are 39 hours to locate, reconnoitre and demolish the chosen target(s)

b) Locks must be reconnoitred in daylight

- The target(s) must be reached by 06:00 hours on the 25th of June.

6. Time/Speed/Distance- the team can move at a speed of 2 mph. Travel is only permitted during hours of darkness (18:00-06:00). Assumes a start time of 18:00 hours on 24th June.

a) From point Y

To	Distance	Time Taken (D/S)	ETA
A	22	11 hours	25th 05:00
B	20	10 hours	25th 04:00

C	22	11 hours	25th 05:00
D	23	11 hours 30 mins	25th 05:30
E	37	18 hours 30 mins	26th 00:30
F	14	7 hours	25th 01:00

- It can be seen that the ETA at Lock E is outside the set time constraint. Therefore, an attack on Lock E will not be considered any further.

b) To point X

From	Distance	Time Taken	ETA
A	68	34 hours	28th 20:00
B	59	29 hours 30 mins	28th 03:30
C	57	28 hours 30 mins	28th 02:30
D	50	25 hours	27th 23:00
F	47	23 hours 30 mins	27th 21:30

OPTIONS

7. There are 3 possible attack options for the waterways problem.

a) Destroy Lock A

b) Destroy Lock B

c) Destroy Lock C & F

8. Destroy Lock A

a) Advantages

   I. Short journey to Lock

   II. Team travels together

   III. Possibility of causing confusion in SENYA if attacks are carried out on the journey back to point X.

b) Disadvantages

   I. Long and tiring journey after the demolition

    II. Heavy enemy presence at the Lock, increasing chance of discovery

    III. Following attack on the Lock the enemy will be alerted and greater chance of discovery en route to point X

9. Destroy Lock B

    a) Advantages

        I. Short journey to demolition

        II. Group travels as a whole

    b) Disadvantages

        I. Long and tiring journey after attack

        II. Substantial enemy patrols, thereby increasing our chances of discovery

        III. Following attack on the Lock the enemy will be alerted and greater chance of discovery en route to point X

10. Destroy Locks C and F

    a) Advantages

        I. 2 locks will be destroyed increasing the SENYA confusion

        II. Enemy does not possess sufficient lifting equipment to repair both locks.

PLANNING EXERCISE 5: EARTHQUAKE RESCUE SOLUTION

IMPORTANT! The following solutions are just examples of a possible way to complete the tasks in hand. They do not represent the most efficient or quickest way to complete the exercise, and should be used for guidance only.

1ST SOLUTION

Time	Description
08:30	• Telephone Cousin in Kinton
	• Explain situation and plan
	• Collect and pack belongings into rucksack
08:35	• Ask Father to take rucksack to your Cousins house
08:40	• Depart Parents house for Fenby (using bike)
08:55	• Arrive at Fenby
	• Collect climbing boots
09:05	• Depart Fenby for Queen Victoria (PH)
09:30	• Arrive at Queen Victoria (PH)
	• Continue to Grangethorpe (using bike)
09:37.5	• Arrive at Grangethorpe
	• Collect medical equipment
At the same time	
08:50	• Father leaves home (using his motorcycle)
	• Carries rucksack
08:59	• Father arrives Kinton (6 mile road)
	• Cousin takes rucksack
	• Cousin walks to Queen Victoria (PH)

Time	Description
09:14	• Cousin arrives at Queen Victoria (PH)
	• Continues onto Grangethorpe Hospital
09:36.5	• Cousin arrives at Grangethorpe Hospital
You	
09:47.5	• Collect medical supplies
	• Meet Cousin outside and collect rucksack
	• Give bike to Cousin
	• Cousin bikes home
	• Walk to Melton bus station
10:17.5	• Arrive at bus station
10:18	• Coach departs

2ND SOLUTION (SAME AS 1ST UNTIL COUSIN ARRIVE AT GRANGETHORPE)

Time	Description
09:36.5	• Cousin arrives at Grangethorpe
09:37.5	• You arrive at Grangethorpe
	• Collect rucksack
	• Ask cousin to walk to Melton bus station
	• Collect medical equipment
09:47.5	• Finish collecting medical equipment
	• Bike towards Melton bus station (with rucksack)
09:52.5	• Catch up with Cousin (5 min at 12 mph = 1 mile)
	• Cousin walking at 4 mph = 1 mile)
	• Cousin takes bike, the bikes home
	• Continue onto Melton bus station
10:07.5	• Arrive at Melton bus station
10:18	• Coach departs

3RD SOLUTION
(FIRST PART OF SOLUTION THE SAME
AS 1ST SOLUTION)

Time	Description
08:59	• Cousin walks to Melton bus station
10:14	• Cousin arrives at Melton bus station
At the same time	
09:47.5	• You depart to Grangethorpe with equipment
09:57.5	• You arrive at Melton bus station
	• Wait for Cousin to arrive
	• Collect rucksack and give him your bike

4TH SOLUTION
(SAME AS 1ST SOLUTION UPTO FENBY)

Time	Description
09:05	• Depart Fenby
	• Bike direct to Melton bus station
09:40	• You arrive at Melton bus station
At the same time	
08:59	• Cousin departs for Kinton by foot with rucksack
09:36.5	• Cousin arrives Grangethorpe
	• Collects medical equipment posing as you (risky!)
09:46.5	• Cousin departs Grangethorpe
10:16.5	• Cousin arrives Melton bus station
	• Collect equipment and rucksack
	• Give bike to Cousin

All these solutions demonstrate that there are numerous possible ways to solve the dilemma. Each solution has attached risks and if the risk does not pay off then the plan is flawed. Therefore, the best solution would be that which has minimal risk and leaves you with as much time to catch the coach as possible. Perhaps leaving the bike outside the shops and hospital for 10 minutes is acceptable especially if the lock is being used to secure it. Make sure your thought process is clear and that you plan for any eventuality.

PLANNING EXERCISE 6: TURKIC DELIGHT SOLUTION

IMPORTANT! The following solutions are just examples of a possible way to complete the tasks in hand. They do not represent the most efficient or quickest way to complete the exercise, and should be used for guidance only.

AIM

From the leader's point of view there are two aims of equal importance. They are:

1. To obtain immediate medical and other assistance for the group including water for the casualties.

2. To notify the other party at HAJI QUSHAN

FACTORS

Time & Space

3. Help can be sought from the British Army at BUKHARA, the police at CHINABAD or the other party at HAJI QUSHAN. Whatever other action is taken, word must be sent to HAJI QUSHAN by 0800 hours 16th July if the expedition is to be saved and water required by 1000 hours at the scene of the accident.

4. Movement on tracks can only be made during the hours of light although roads can be used at night. No man should travel alone.

5. First light 0500; last light 1900 hours

Routes

6. To DAMLA

Route	Distance	Time	Day	ETA	Remarks
Track to Damla	5 miles	2½ hours		19:00	Start 16:30 hrs, must reach Damla by last light to avoid night stop
Road: Damla to Army base	27 miles	10 hours	Day 1	05:00	Time includes a 1 hour rest. Army break camp 07:00 hours
Vehicle: Army camp to Damla	27 miles	54 mins	Day 1	05:54	
Damla-Accident	5 miles	1 hour	Day 1	06:54	
TOTAL	**64 miles**	**14 h 24 m**			

7. To HAJI QUSHAN

Route	Distance	Time	Day	ETA	Remarks
By track to road	8 miles	4 hours + 10 hours	Day 1	06:30	Enforced night stop
By road to HAJI QUSHAN	3 miles	1 hour	Day 1	07:30	Must reach HAJI QUSHAN by 08:00
Vehicle to accident	11 miles	2 h 12m	Day 1	09:42	
TOTAL	**22 miles**	**17 h 12 m**			

8. To CHINABAD

Route	Distance	Time	Day	ETA	Remarks
By track	17 miles	8½ hours +10 hours	Day 1	11:00	Enforced night stop
Return by vehicle	17 miles	3h 24m	Day 1	14:24	
TOTAL	**34 miles**	**21 h 24m**			

9. HAJI QUSHAN to CHINABAD

Route	Distance	Time	Day	ETA	Remarks
On foot	25 miles	8 h 20 m	Day 1	16:00+	
By vehicle	25 miles	50 mins	Day 1	08:30	
TOTAL	**50 miles**	**9 h 10 m**			

OTHER FACTORS

10. The leader cannot rely on the already unreliable vehicle being serviceable before day 1 09:00 hours and this a much later time than help can be obtained from the British Army Base.

11. Drinking water must be obtained for Parry and Kelly by day 1 10:00 hours. This means that to go to CHINABAD is ruled out and that there is a risk in going to HAJI QUSHAN only.

12. The British Army base is probably able to react more quickly to cas-evac Parry and there is a good chance that some medical advice will be available at the camp. There will also be no language problems.

SUGGESTED PLAN

13. The leader briefs the group and sends two fit members of the group to BUKHARA via DAMLA. They have just under 2 ½ hours of daylight left and should reach DAMLA before last light. This will enable them to continue the journey to BUKHARA through the night, using the road. They will take no water with them as they can obtain water from DAMLA.

14. The injured man, the mechanic and Kelly, who will not be fit enough to travel any distance on foot, will stay with the vehicle until help arrives. Once the medical student has attended to Parry, he and the leader of the group will set out for HAJI QUSHAN. They will take half a pint of water between them as they should be at their destination before thirst becomes a serious problem. They will travel light but take warm clothing for the overnight stop. The will halt as soon as it becomes impossible to see their way and will remain on the track until first light; they will then proceed with all possible speed to HAJI QUSHAN. They must arrive at the track-road junction by 08:00 hours in order to intercept the other party who should be leaving HAJI QUSHAN at that time.

15. The pair travelling to BUKHARA must arrive at the British Army base before 07:00 hours as this is the scheduled time of the troops' departure. If help is immediately forthcoming, ETA of the rescue party at the scene of the accident will be 07:00 hours

16. If the pair going to HAJI QUSHAN makes contact with the other party, they return by transport, assuming that the track is usable for vehicle. If the track is unusable for vehicles the leader of the other party must send a selected group on foot, with such assistance as can be provided.

17. If no contact is made with the other party, the pair will remain at HAJI QUSHAN until 12:00 hours. If, by that time, they have received no message from their own group they will proceed, as swiftly as possible, to CHINABAD to inform the police.

ALTERNATIVE COURSES OF ACTION

18. The new leader may decide to disregard the possibility of other help and to rely solely on the party at HAJI QUSHAN for assistance. This is living dangerous and the plan should be assessed accordingly. Even if the other group is available it will not be able to provide the skilled medical aid which is needed and an approach will have to be made to the police at CHINABAD for assistance. This will take much longer to provide and thus the plan, in addition to its overall defect, suffers also from a lack of urgency.

19. A plan which relies on using the track from DAMLA to notify the police at CHINABAD disregards the time factor. Any plan which omits action to notify the group at HAJI QUSHAN fails to achieve the complete aim. A plan which keeps the whole group inactive overnight in the hope that the vehicle will be usable the next morning should be severely marked down.

20. Under no circumstances should be two ill members of the group be left on their own.

PLANNING EXERCISE 7: COLUMBUS COUNTDOWN SOLUTION

IMPORTANT! The following solutions are just examples of a possible way to complete the tasks in hand. They do not represent the most efficient or quickest way to complete the exercise, and should be used for guidance only.

AIM

Get the party to a safe location and provide medical attention for MEREDITH as possible.

FACTORS

1. MANUEL may attack a static party of any size anytime

2. When over 2 miles from the hideout by track or path he will not attack a party on the move more than twice his size. We just make that (9 versus 16 males, 2 females, 1 child, 1 crew)

3. One of your party, MEREDITH, is ill and must reach a doctor as soon as possible

4. Deductions

    a) We cannot stay at the crash site

    b) When we move we must keep moving

    c) We must head for one of the villages in order to get medical aid

    d) Provided that we do keep moving and have not met MANUEL we are safe once we have passed

        I. 1 miles EAST of Point A if heading to VICTORIA

        II. Point B if heading for COLUMBO

        III. Point Y if heading for GARCIA

Time & Space

a) Actual time

   I. We left HEATHROW at 06:00 hours GMT = 07:00 hours local time

   II. Crashed after 5 hours flying = 1200 hours local time

   III. Spent ½ hour from the crash dealing with shepherd = 1230 hours local time

   IV. ½ hour to plan and brief party = 1300 hours local time

Deduction: We will be ready to move at 1300 hours local time. (All timings will be local time from now on)

b) Time from the Crash Site to the Villages

Village	Point Y	Point E	Point B	Point C	ETA
VICTORA	14:00 hrs (1)	15:00 hrs			17:00 hrs (2)
COLUMBO	14:00 hrs (1)		15:00 hrs		18:00 hrs (3)
GARCIA	14:00 hrs (1)			16:00 hrs	18:30 hrs (4)

Note:

   I. ½ mile path at ½ mph = 1 hour

   II. 1 hr (1) + 1 mile track at 1 mph (1 hr) + 4 miles road at 2 mph (2 hrs) = Total 4 hours

   III. 1 hr (1) + 1 mile track at 1 mph (1 hr) + 6 miles road at 2 mph (3 hrs) = Total 5 hours

   IV. 1 hr (1) + 2 mile track at 1 mph (2 hr) + 5 miles road at 2 mph (2½ hrs) = Total 5½ hours

a) Manuel's Times- if he is at his hideout as soon as he returns from VICTORIA at 1330 hours

   I. To point Y via direct path: 2 miles at 2 mph (1hr) = 14:30 hours

II. To crash site (point X) 1 hour to point Y + ½ mile path at 1 mph (½ hour) = 15:00 hours

III. To point A: 1 mile path at 1 mph (1 hr) = 14:30 hours

IV. To point B: 2 mile path at 1 mph (2 hr) = 15:30 hours

V. To point D: 2 mile path at 1 mph (2 hr) = 15:30 hours

Deductions:

a)   We can be at Point Y (14:00 hours), which we must get to whichever route is chosen before Manuel (14:30 hours)

b)   Manuel can get to the crash site (Point X) ¼ hour before the helicopter, which arrives 15:15 hours (3¼ from the crash time at 1200 hours). We therefore cannot leave Meredith plus 2 others to be evacuated by the helicopter

c)   If Manuel makes directly for either Point A or Point B, he arrives before our party, should we take the route that he has chosen to ambush.

AVAILABLE OPTIONS

1.   VICTORIA: Although this is the quickest route, it is also the most dangerous.

2.   COLUMBO: Quicker than GARCIA, but only half an hour. The risk of attack at Point D should Manuel follow us from Point Y is high and if he does pick on Point D as our ambush point we are done for. Only safe is he picks the wrong ambush point and goes to Point A.

3.   GARCIA: It will take longer to get MEREDITH to a doctor and it is possible that the extra half an hour could be critical. It is, however, completely safe as far as Manuel is concerned, provided we keep on moving.

Deductions:

a)   VICTORIA: Discounted

b)   COLUMBO: The risks are too great. I could lose the whole party for the sake of half an hour

c)   GARCIA: My chosen option, being the only sure safe route

PLAN

5. General Outline: We are to travel together as one party to GARCIA

6. Helicopter: We will take the flare gun with us. If the pilot sees our tracks in the snow he may follow us, or we may be able to attract his attention with a flare. We would be between Point Y and Point C at this time and MEREDITH some 3 hours earlier than on foot. This, however, would be a bonus and not essential part of the plan.

7. Timings:

A. Time of departure from Point X – 13:00 hours

B. Arrive Point Y – 14:00 hours

C. Arrive Point C – 16:00 hours

D. ETA GARCIA – 18:30 hours

PLANNING EXECISE 8: BAY BLAZE SOLUTION

IMPORTANT! The following solutions are just examples of a possible way to complete the tasks in hand. They do not represent the most efficient or quickest way to complete the exercise, and should be used for guidance only.

AIM

To alert the Park Fire Warden as soon as possible and to clear and evacuate the area by 1300 hours.

FACTORS

People and Places

1. Tower Springs: 2 Hikers possibly in the area

Deduction: Must search this area to alert them

2. Sister Lakes: Son and his friend fishing here.

Deduction: Fire will reach this area first. Hence they are in the most danger and must be alerted first.

3. Fox Cottage: 3 people (1 injured, 1 young, 1 elderly). Vacated here without a vehicle. The house has a telephone.

4. Thumb Farm: Me, 2 hikers and a tractor (with equipment attached) located here.

Deduction: Hikers could be used to help raise alarm. I know the area well therefore can search quicker.

5. Wife: Travelling from Pebble Creek to Fox cottage in Ford Estate car. Expected to pass Thumb Bridge between 1200-1230 hours

Deduction: Must be stopped from going to Fox Cottage. Somebody needs to stop her at Thumb Bridge. Ford can be used as transport once stopped.

Transport

1. 4 × 4: At Sister Lakes

Deduction: Largest capacity (10) and fastest transport available. Must get there ASAP.

2. Tractor: At farm

Deduction: Slow but faster than walking. Quickest means of transport from farm. Quicker with equipment detached but this takes time.

3. Boat: In Boat shed on this side of the Lake.

Deduction: Could use this to save driving around the Lake. Makes walking to the cottage a possibility.

Time and Space

1. Fire will dictate all time and space. 3mph in SW direction, now 1 mile NE of Fishing Bridge

2. By 10:30 hours= fire at eastern lake of sister lakes.

Deduction:

Must go there before 10:30 hours to rescue son

Hikers (possibly) at the Tower Springs also in imminent danger. Must search this area too.

These areas are the priorities

3. By 11:30 hours = fire at head of Thumb Lake

Deduction: Must be clear of this area by this time

4. By 12:30 hours = Fire at edge of Fox Cottage area

Deduction: Must have evacuated 3 people in cottage by this time

5. By 13:00 hours = fire will reach area containing sheep (River Pelican may slow fire ETA)

Deduction: Must try to save them (as lowest priority) if have time

Distances

1. Farm to Cottage

    a) Walking – boat – walking

3 miles to lake	= 1 hour walk
Boat	= 15 minutes
Cottage	= 10 minutes
Total time	**= 1 hour 25 minutes**

    b) Tractor-boat-walking

5 mph	= 36 minutes to lake
Total time	= 1 hour 1 minute
Take off equipment	= 30 minutes
At 10 mph to lake	= 18 minutes
Total time	**= 1 hour 13 minutes**

Deductions:

    I. Tractor with equipment is fastest method of getting to the cottage

    II. However, with time taken, the fire will have already reached Tower Springs and the Sister Lakes before you can alert.

    III. Therefore must split party at farm and use tractor to alert sister lakes

    IV. Cottage reached by 1055 hours by walking/boat.

2. Farm to Sister Lakes

Latest possible ETA 1020 hours (allowing for 10 minute's walk to vehicle)

    a) Tractor + equipment = 2 miles at 5 mph = 24 minutes + 10 minute's walk

Total time	**= 34 minutes**
ETA	**= 10:04 hours**

    b) Tractor – equipment = 30 minutes + 2 miles at 10 mph

        = 30 + 12 + 10 = 52 minutes

        ETA = 10:22 hours

c) Walking = 2 miles at 3 mph = 40 minutes + 10 minutes =
50 minutes

ETA = 10:20 Hours

Deductions:

I. Fastest method = tractor + equipment

II. Walking allows no time to get to Falls

3. Lake to Tower Springs

10 minutes + 2 miles at 10 mph (4 × 4) = 10 + 12 = 22 minutes

ETA = 10:26 Hours

Deductions

I. Little time to conduct search if hikers not at springs.

II. Tractor at 5 mph would take 24 minutes – too late

4. Farm to Tower Springs

4 miles at 5 mph = 48 minutes (tractor with equipment)

ETA = 10:26 Hours

Deductions:

I. Leaves 12 minutes to search and evacuate

4 miles at 10 mph = 30 minutes + 24 minutes
(tractor without equipment)

II. Slower. Leaves only 6 minutes to search area.

5. Farm to Thumb Bridge (16 miles)

4 × 4 20 mph = 48 minutes

Tractor with equipment 5 mph = 3 hours 12 minutes

Tractor without equipment 10 mph = 1 hr 36 mins + 30 minutes
(2hrs 6 mins)

Deductions: Latest departure time from farm is 11:22 hours to alert wife.

6. Thumb Bridge to Cottage

5 miles road, 3.5 miles track.

4 × 4: 5 miles at 20 mph

= 15 minutes + 3½ at 10 mph = 21 mins

Total time = 36 minutes

Deductions:

I. Latest departure from bridge to cottage 11:44 hours. To be safe 11:26 hours allow more time to load them into the 4 × 4.

II. Tractor too slow (cannot carry passengers)

III. Cannot rely on wife's car as no definitive ETA. Must use own facilities.

7. Sheep

a) 7 miles from farm. At a pace of 3 mph would take (self or son) 2 hours 20 minutes to drive back to the farm.

b) Route out (from farm): 2 miles road, 5 miles

1) 4 × 4 = 2 miles at 20 mph = 6 minutes + 5 miles at 10 mph = 30 minutes.

2) Tractor with equipment at 5 mph = 1 hour 24 minutes

3) Tractor without equipment at 10 mph = 42 minutes + 30 minutes = 1 hour 12 minutes

Deductions:

I. Quickest round trip 2 hours 56 minutes with 4 × 4 or 3 hours 32 minutes with tractor

II. Must evacuate sheep by 13:00 hours therefore must leave farm by 10:04 hours in 4 × 4 or 09:28 hours in tractor.

III. Neither of these options are possible unless son and friends arrive back at farm on own initiative (this cannot be relied upon)

IV. It is unlikely that the sheep will be rescued.

POSSIBLE PLAN

1. Instruct hikers to walk to boat shed and head across lake to alert fire warden using phone at fox cottage and await with family for rescue. Drive tractor (with equipment) to Sister Lakes, to rescue son & friend. Abandon tractor, with son and friend drive 4 × 4 on to Tower Springs, search and rescue 2 hikers. Son drives all in 4 × 4 past farm to Thumb Bridge – drop hikers on the bridge to flag down Ford Estate. 4 × 4 continues to cottage to rescue others and takes everyone to Bay Bridge.

BREAKDOWN OF POSSIBLE PLAN DEPART 09:30HRS

Hikers

1. Hikers walk to lake 3 miles 1 hour (10:30hrs)

2. Boat across lake 15 minutes (10:45hrs)

3. Walk to cottage 10 minutes (10:55hrs)

Myself

1. Tractor to Sister lakes 2 miles + 10 minute walk (10:04hrs)

2. 10 minute walk, then 4 × 4, 2 miles to tower springs (10:22hrs)

3. Tower Springs to Thumb bridge 4 miles at 10 mph, 16 miles at 20 mph (11:36hrs)

4. Thumb bridge to Fox Cottage 5 miles at 20 mph, 3.5 miles at 10 mph (12:12hrs)

5. Fox Cottage to bay bridge 3.5 miles at 10 mph, 9 miles at 20 mph (13:02hrs)